THE

CHILDREN'S WAR -

1939-1945

An anthology in verse of one child's

experiences of war

Archie Cameron

Archie Cameron's website :

www.archiecameronnovels.com

The photo in the dedication is presented as it was found in the wreckage of our house.

Dedicated to my sisters Jeane Wood and Margaret Hammond the sibling evacuees.

CONTENTS

PAGE

ix

x

1. ON HEARING THE FIRST SIREN IN AUTUMN – 1939. (With apologies to Delius)

The first wail of a siren came

On a mild September day

Mother was hanging out washing

And I was out to play

Sitting in my new red racing car

A shrill noise filled the air

A warbling, wailing cacophony

That I could hardly bear

Looking up at Mother

I asked what was all that din

Mother' face as she hung the clothes

Just broadened with a grin

'It's only a test siren luv

-- so we know what to expect.

-- they announced it on the radio

-- certainly gives the right effect.'

That noise became so scary

When later it would sound

We'd rush down to the shelter

To safety underground

But when the 'All clear' sounded

It was always a relief

It meant a raid was over

But not the suffering or the grief

2. EVACUATION- WINTER 1939/1940

Out of the fog filled London streets

And no time to complain

Labelled, checked for our gas mask box

And herded on a train

A journey through the countryside

Arriving at Uckfield town

Where people waited to choose a child

Kind strangers smiling down

At upturned faces full of fear

Where would we sleep tonight?

Perhaps a place that was quite near

It soon would be alright

But we were left there all alone

My two big sisters and me

All the others on their way to a new home

and their tea.

Then a vicar came across and gave a toothy smile

'It won't be long we'll fix you up just wait a little while'

The while became an hour or so before we were taken in

By two spinsters who volunteered their place

And with a kindly grin led us to their cottage

And bid us three go in

They suffered us for just one week

Soon we were on our way

To a dairy farmers house

Where this time we hoped we stay

But the farmer could only accommodate one

So the next day close to noon

We were driven off to Nutley

In a huge Rolls Royce saloon

Accommodated for the rest of the year

In a country house with trees

And so we stayed together

We sibling evacuees.

3. WATCHING A DOG-FIGHT - SUMMER 1940.

The summer days in Nutley

We're always filled with fun

On the heath we took our ease

Just laying in the sun

When suddenly the sky was filled

With whirling, twirling planes

Long vapour trails criss-crossed the sky

I gazed up wishing I could fly

Among those fluffy lanes.

The battle lasted for a while

Then the aircraft flew away

We all stood up and raised a cheer

Old 'Jerry' had been chased from here

Spitfires had won the day.

4. A VISIT TO THE DENTIST – 1940

I was suffering from toothache

So our host arranged one day

For a visit to the dentist

In a town not far away

I was taken by the Chauffeur

In the Rolls Royce limousine

Although I had no option

And wasn't very keen

I arrived at the dentist's surgery

And was placed in the dentist's chair

He did a quick inspection

Taking a lot of care

And then he said. 'We'll take that out'

And turned to grab a mask

Which he placed upon my mouth and nose

And started on his task

By dripping something on the gauze

Soon I was passing out

From then I don't remember

T'ill the dentist gave a shout

'You alright young man it's over now'

There was a gap where my tooth had been

And although there was no pain now

I was feeling rather green

I thought I might be sick right there

So I was helped back to the car

The Chauffeur said we'd get back quick

It wasn't very far

And he didn't want me vomiting

In this lovely automobile

So he handed me a paper bag

In case I might be ill

We made it back to Nutley

Without a bad mishap

But I spent the rest of that testing day

With my head in my sister's lap

So my first trip to the dentist

Was certainly not my choice

But who can say their transport there

Was an elegant Rolls Royce

5. HOME AGAIN – AUTUMN 1940

Our stay at the house in Nutley

Was suddenly to end

Why such an awful thing should happen

We couldn't comprehend

Our Lady host's companion

Who had looked after us so well

Had a husband in the RAF

And as far as we could tell

He was an officer at Biggin Hill

When enemy planes overhead

Bombed the RAF Station

Leaving many injured and dead

He was among the people killed

There was nothing we could say

My mother felt we had to go

It was impossible to stay

For she realised our friend needed time

To be alone and grieve

To come to terms with this tragic loss

So we sadly took our leave

Saying farewell to the friends we made

Many tears were shed by us

When Mother came to pick us up

And we left on a Green Line bus

It was a sad departure

From that beautiful country place

Back to a foggy wintry London

Knowing nothing of what we would face

6. INCIDENT IN LEWISHAM HIGH STREET - SEPTEMBER 1940

High Street was a bustling place

Where Mother went to shop

Along busy lines of market stalls

No war could ever stop

How far would coupons go this week?

What were the priorities

Perhaps two ounces of fresh butter

Or a tiny lump of cheese

For some scraggy meat for supper

My mother used to queue

And buy tins of dried milk and powdered eggs

To last a week or two.

Few sweeties for me to enjoy

No fruit from far away lands

But there was a nice sweet candy twist

Pressed into my eager hands

Soon it was time set off home

About a mile away

Suddenly sirens sounded

We hurried without delay

Then I heard a rumble

And appearing from the east

A flight of 'Jerry' Bombers came

Like some droning, moaning beast

Mother reached the railway bridge

Not showing any fear

Found a stack of sandbags

And pushed me to the rear

Suddenly without warning

A bomber dived and strafed the street

Firing without conscience

Bullets hit the ground like sleet

As people screamed and bullets struck

I was protected by my Mother

Cowering behind that sandbagged wall

Using her body as a cover

Protecting me amid the strife

Of bombers overhead

Causing chaos, taking life

Leaving injured, scarred and dead

We had both survived the raid

Among the fear and grief

But behind the protecting sand bagged wall

Mother shaking like a leaf

Soon the 'all clear' sounded

29

We were helped out by some strangers

My Mother had a tale to tell

Wartime shopping had its dangers.

7. A NEW HOBBY - COLLECTING SHRAPNEL – WINTER 1940

We would always look for shrapnel

When we went along the lanes

Little bits of metal

From exploded bombs and planes

I kept mine in a shoe box

But mother said one day

I should stop that craze at once

It was a dangerous game to play

She said that Nazi aircraft

Were dropping little things

That looked just like a butterfly

With little metal wings

And if I ever touched one

It was likely to explode

And I'd end up dead or injured

In the middle of some road

Heeding mother's warning

(For she was always right)

I swopped my old shoe box of bits

For an incendiary bomb tail flight.

(And I still have it after all these years)

8. BOMBED OUT - WINTER 1940

Just another night of blitz

Following 'Winnie the Warbler's' shrill refrain

Droning bombers flown by Fritz

Were dropping bombs like rain

We settled down in our Anderson

As the crump of bombs drew near

No chance of any sleep for us

My Grandma shook with fear

And mother trying to calm us

Held us oh so near

'No one is going to harm you

...not while I am here'

The noise of bombs grew louder

Falling from those darkened skies

An explosion lifted the shelter up

And dust got in our eyes

'God that was near.' My mother gasped.

My Grandma screamed and cried

'Sounds like our next door neighbour's house

...I hope they're not inside'

The bombers passed right overhead

And a new noise we could hear

A kind of heavy crackling sound

It seemed so very near

My mother held us tightly

'We all must stay safe in here

…we shouldn't go outside at all

...until we hear 'all clear' '

And very near to daybreak

When we couldn't take much more

Came an anxious voice. 'Alright inside?'

Shouted loudly through the door

I recognised my father's voice

Who'd been away for days

As Chief Warden of an area

The Bombers tried to raze

My mother poked her head outside

And to her great dismay

Our house had received a direct hit

Roof and walls were blown away

A raging fire was eating up

The remains of what we had

After that long night of bombing

We felt so tired and sad

I was very angry

For just like any boys

Uppermost in my mind

Was the fact I'd lost my toys

Sent to safety to a Buckinghamshire town

And with a heavy heart

My mother just broke down in tears

We were safe, she'd played her part.

(Photo of the siblings recovered from our blitzed house hence I have retained the condition).

9. TO SAFETY IN SHROPSHIRE - WINTER 1940

At last my Dad was posted

By a War Office communique

He said goodbye to all of us

And soon he went away

Just a short time after

We received a call one night

To join him up in Shropshire

Where the family would unite

We boarded a train at Paddington

Shropshire bound at last

We children so excited

As towns went whizzing past

But as the night descended

Shutters blocked our view

Mum said 'it's just the blackout

-the train has to blackout too.'

The journey became a slow one

We stopped many times that night and day

Because of enemy action

Avoiding raids along the way

Arriving early morning

Wellington town a welcome sight

We alighted with all our cases

After travelling through the eventful night

There my father waited anxiously

Grinning like a Cheshire Cat

And as at last he saw us

He waved his Trilby hat

He led us from the station

To our lodgings in the town

Our landlady welcomed us at the door

'Come in and sit you down.

…You must be tired the kettles on

…I'll make a cup of tea

…Welcome to my humble home.

I'm Mrs Blakely'

Now safe from all the bombing

We were soon to settle in

To a new life there in Shropshire

New adventures to begin.

10. LEARNING TO LIVE WITH THE BASIC ESSENTIALS – EARLY 1941

It was a quite new experience

At our lodgings in the town

The accommodation very sparse

Three rooms up and down

And just an outside toilet

Up the garden a few paces

No bathroom just the scullery

To wash our mucky faces

And bath time was a ritual

The tin bath would come out

Mum boiled the kettle on the range

And filled it from the spout

When the right mix was achieved

We'd climb in one after the other

Then our backs and fronts were washed

Scrubbed vigorously by my mother

And when the ritual was over

We climb up stairs to bed

With a candlestick to guide us

Lighting every tread

And sometimes on a winter's morning

We'd wake up to the sight

Of beautiful patterns made of Ice

Formed on window panes overnight

No electric lights with switches

In the ground floor rooms at night

Just gas lights with a mantle

With a chain to pull to light

And with a pop they came to life

To light our little world

A warm glow filled the room

As on the sofa we three curled

So that was our introduction to Shropshire

In those first wartime years

But it was a lovely safe warm haven

Away from London's fears

11. A SUDDEN REDUNDANCY - EARLY 1941

My Grandad arrived in Shropshire

He looked forlorn and tired

He'd been at his job in the City

But he said he'd just been fired

He said it was just a little joke

As he drunk a cup of tea

The bombs had destroyed his place of work

The wharf at Brewer's Quay

He'd worked there since 1926

And had hardly missed a day

Looking after security

Around the shipping bay

As a former City Policeman

The City was his life

And now the enemy aircraft

Had brought misery and strife

He had no job to go to

Brewer's Quay destroyed

Just a damaged burnt out shell

I could see he was annoyed

For he was sixty five years old

And hoping to retire

And the job and income he had earned

Had been destroyed by fire

I suddenly saw the funny side

Of his opening remark

It was right he had been fired

But by an incendiary spark

But we learned later what he'd done

On that night of terrible strife

When the Wharf went up flames

He had risked his very life

A cat with kittens trapped inside

The warehouse now alight

He went back inside and rescued them

On that fateful night

And he never mentioned a word of this

Though he received a minor burn

Cat and kittens were OK

Now we welcomed his safe return

12. HOSPITALIZED - SPRING 1941

I was diagnosed with infantile paralysis

In 1941

And sent to Gobowen hospital

Where my treatment was begun

The paralysis had touched both my legs

Particularly my right

I was six and very frightened

Especially at night

I spent many months confined there

A lot of time alone

In a vast and empty ward

With little news of home

My parent's visits were restricted

But once a month they tried

I would be so pleased to see them

Many times I cried

Suddenly in the summer

The ward was quickly filled

With soldiers wounded at the front

Relieved they'd not been killed

I soon became their mascot

They missed their families so

And I reminded them of home

Where they wished they could go

The months went by so quickly

Physiotherapy would prove

With water exercise and massage

I could make my poor legs move

At last my treatment over

With plastered legs went home

Then many painful years would pass

Before I'd stand alone

(Dedicated to those doctors and nurses of the

Robert Jones and Dame Agnes Hunt
Orthopaedic Hospital Oswestry. With their help I
went on to play Rugby at Adam's Grammar
school, for Newport Town and Service Teams,
became a Sea Cadet won whaler boat races did
many physical courses at sea and served in the
Royal Marines Commandos and the Police
Service)

13. RETURN FROM HOSPITAL –
WINTER 1941

Before I had left hospital

I was told one day

My family had move to a new house

At Donnington miles away

Many new houses were being built

Close to a Military store

Where my father was employed

Full of spare parts for the war

The house was quite unusual

The roof had a flat top

There was plenty of accommodation

All our family could stop

So when I returned to the new house

I was surprised at all the fuss

But happy that Grandma and Grandad

Would be living there with us

A family united

And with tender loving care

It was the best medicine for me

After all I had to bear

14. PERIODS OF PAIN - 1941/42

For months after my discharge

My legs were plaster bound

Casts from my feet to the top of my thigh

So I couldn't get around

Every month they were renewed

Until at last one day

The casts were reduced to below the knee

And I could stand and play

A tiny problem soon occurred

When a penny I tried to hide

Slipped out of my fumbling fingers

And I lost it down the side

I didn't tell my Parents

I thought they'd have a fit

But when the right leg was exposed

A green patch covered it

The nurse retrieved my penny

As she cut the cast away

But Mother gave me a piece of her mind

For the shock she had that day

Eventually when the plasters went

Supported by leg iron frames

Fitted to help to brace the legs

It didn't stop the pains

They continued almost constantly

As I started again to walk

My parents would converse

About ways to help me walk

For them it was just common sense

To give massage day or night

Whenever the pain got so intense

And they heard my sorry plight

So for nearly two years

My parents eased the pain

Spending hours massaging my legs

Until I went to sleep again

This is a tribute to the efforts

My parents would employ

When pain so overwhelming

Affected their small boy

15. FIRST DAY AT A NEW SCHOOL – 1942

Now I was back from hospital

It was time to go to school

So we went off to an interview

I felt a perfect fool

For I was transported in a large push chair

My mother pushing me

We were seeing the headmistress

At Donnington Wood C of E

We were ushered to the office

The headmistress Mrs Hughes

Explained the layout of the school

And the class that she would choose

Then she came over to me

And with a little grin

She said 'Don't worry you will soon make

friends'

But I kicked her in the shin

My mother was dumbfounded

Embarrassed and alarmed

She apologised to the head teacher

And hoped she wasn't harmed

But the head teacher was a gentle type

And said she understood

When I had settled into the school

She knew I would be good

She offered Mum a cup of tea

And the interview was ended

But when later we got home

My behaviour could not be defended

I had the biggest telling off

For that unruly act

And if I wasn't in a push chair

My bottom would be smacked

I never forgot that interview

From then I kept the rule

And later on in my last year

Passed the exam for Grammar school

16. INITIATION CEREMONY – SPRING 1942

One day in May I was approached

To join a gang of boys

Our ages were from eight and ten

All fed up playing with toys

We wanted to do more adventurous things

Like climbing trees and hills

And though I still wore leg irons

I was attracted by the thrills

But first I had to pass a test

In an initiation ceremony

By grabbing a fresh nettle

And climbing up a tree

I was happy with the nettle

Though it made my poor hand itch

When next I had a tree to climb

There was an unseen hitch

One of the leg irons snapped in two

Whilst climbing up the tree

With my right leg unsupported

Soon I was falling free

I landed in a heap of leaves

The boys all gathered round

Very glad to see that I

Was reasonably safe and sound

But I passed the initiation

A chum helped me on my way

But I never told my Mother

How the leg iron broke that day

17. GANG WARFARE – SPRING/SUMMER 1942

Children rarely understand

About making a fresh new start

Our presence in the district

Kept us strangers quite apart

From local children in the neighbourhood

Who couldn't understand

The sudden influx of Londoners

Into their green and pleasant land

Inevitably fights had broken out

Between opposing gangs

Some were very nasty

Leaving lots of knocks and bangs

But gradually the tension broke

Among those we would deride

Many friendships were soon made

With the kids on the other side

And as the years began to pass

From those fateful days of war

Friendships turned to marriage

And prejudice was no more

Although they never forgot their roots

At least it can be said

Their children and grandchildren

Are Shropshire born and bred

18. RADIO TIMES - 1939/1945 AND BEYOND

Radio was a Godsend

When favourite programmes would begin

It kept our young minds off the War

When peace was caving in

By the fireplace we'd sit listening

To the dear old BBC

Our source of entertainment

Every evening after tea

We had an old Pye radio

In a brown wood cabinet

On the front was a fret sawn sunrise

And on the side the knobs were set

And when switched ON we'd settle

And patiently we'd wait

For 'Children's Hour with Uncle Mac'

And 'Monday Night at Eight'

Sandy Macpherson on the organ

Tommy Handley's ITMA crew

Band Wagon and Arthur Askey

Hi Gang with Ben Lyon too

It gave us 'Music While You Work'

The latest hits would play

A welcome visit by 'Workers Playtime'

Kept factories working night and day

We had plenty of variety

Plombley's 'Desert Island Discs'

And Vera Lynn and Ann Shelton

Sang in foreign places taking risks

John Snagge, Frank Phillips and Alvar Liddell

Kept us up to date each day

With the fighting at the front

In a war so far away

And every Tuesday afternoon

We'd run down to the shop

Carrying the spare accumulator

With sixpence for a swop

Without a charged accumulator

The radio wouldn't work

So this was a weekly chore

We children couldn't shirk

The radio kept us smiling

Throughout those days of fear

When hope was almost fading

We kept the radio near

And so we spent our evenings

In the dark days of the war

Listening to the radio

From a world beyond our door

19. WATCHING AIR RAIDS OVER
THE BLACK COUNTRY - AUTUMN 1942

Bombs rained down on the Midlands

That cold and frosty night

We kids had gone out for a stroll

And the winter sky seemed bright

As we came to the old 'Four Ways'

The eastern sky was glowing red

The area was taking a pounding

And fires were beginning to spread

And we so many miles away

From where bombers took no pity

Watched this glowing night sky

Lighting up a burning City

We gazed in awe this spectacle

Till it became too cold to stay

My big sister took us by the hand

And said as she led us away

'Those poor souls are in trouble but

-there's nothing we can do

-but pray that they can keep safe

-and reach their homes like you'.

And now it's a vivid memory

Of a fiery glowing sky

And wondering how out of all that strife

The 'Black Country' folk got by.

20. SUNDAY SCHOOL AND AFTER - 1942/44

On Sunday it was our duty

To attend our Sunday School

At St Mathews Parish Church

To learn the Christian rule

As we would reach the church door

Waiting on the entrance seat

The church warden Jabus Stevens

Sucking a Rennie sweet

The Rennie white formed around his lips

And with a chalky grin

He'd open up the church doors

And bid us all go in

Clutching our Sunday School stamp books

We'd sit along the pews

Listening to the Teacher

Telling us the Good News

Then a stamp for our attendance

Which we stuck into our book

To prove to Mother that we'd been to church

Not playing near the brook

And after the Sunday sermonising

It was our custom all to go

To watch films in the AOS canteen

At an afternoon picture show

Now in the canteen of the Ordnance Depot

We children safe from danger

Watched films of Laurel and Hardy

Roy Rodgers and Lone Ranger

Returning home it was sometimes dark

So pinned to our coats and macs

Our phosphorescent badges

We thought would light our tracks

And that's how we spent our Sundays

In those dark wartime days

With Christian text and film stars

To set our minds ablaze

21. AIR RAID DRILL – 1942

An air raid shelter had been built

On the front of our school green

And once a month we'd have a drill

We were always very keen

Because every time it happened

We'd miss an hour in class

The bell would ring and we'd form up

And file out on the grass

One by one we'd enter

This long dark concrete place

Sit along the wooden benches

Staring face to face

With pupils from other classes

All chattering with each other

Some little ones were frightened

77

And shouted for their mother

The teachers there would hold their hand

And popular songs we'd sing

Like 'Roll out the Barrel'

Then once again the bell would ring

And we'd file back to our classrooms

Our air raid drill now ended

We'd settle down to lessons

Our brief escape suspended

'Till the next time the bell would ring

For another air raid drill to face

And an escape from our lessons

Down to that long dark concrete place

22. ACK ACK GUNS ARRIVE ON OUR GREEN - 1942

Walking down to the shops one day

At Donnington Parade

Two huge guns had appeared on the green

And what a sight they made

A soldier said when we kids asked

That they were here to stay

And if they saw old 'Jerry'

They'd be fired without delay

He explained these were Ack Ack guns

And if the enemy approached our town

They'd open up with everything

And shoot the 'buggers' down

He apologised for swearing

In front of all us boys

But he said we'd know when those guns fired

We'd certainly hear the noise

We thanked him and went shopping

Later told Mum what we'd seen

About huge pieces of artillery

Defending our small green

23. THE CHRISTMAS PARTY - 1942

We children were so excited

An invitation we had seen

We were going to a Christmas Party

In the AOS Canteen

Soon the great day had arrived

An accompanied by our Mum

We headed off to the Party

Hoping all our friends would come

We sat down to a lovely tea

With jelly cakes and such

It wasn't long before we found

We'd eaten far too much

And after the table was cleared away

Our spirits had a lift

Father Christmas entered

And gave us all a gift

I received a railway engine

On each corner a bright green wheel

The boiler was a dried milk tin

And the chimney a cotton reel

It was painted in GWR green

With lots of golden stripes

I was so excited

I said to my Mum later 'Cripes

…this is the best present I have had

…since I lost all my toys I think

I thanked old Father Christmas

And he gave me a cheery wink

I treasured the engine till it fell apart

After many, many years

Even though I was far too old

I was reduced to tears

And as we left that Christmas treat

And went out through the door

Mum told me who made that special train'

It was a German Prisoner of War

24. THE YANKS ARE HERE – SPRING 1943

In the fresh Spring days of '43

A rumour spread afar

That troops in a different uniform

Had been seen in a local bar

We soon found out from father

US soldiers had moved quite near

Quite a large detachment

With all their heavy gear

We shouted, 'Got any gum chum'

Whenever they came in sight

Occasionally we get a Hershey Bar

And they always so polite

A club was built behind our Parade of shops

which they went most days

And there to our astonishment

They installed the latest craze

Playing the current records

For everyone to hear

A shiny sparkling Juke Box

Made us gather round and cheer

There was Frank Sinatra crooning

Lovely Dinah Shore would sing

And Louis Armstrong's gravely voice

With The Andrew Sisters and Bing

And lots of great dance music

Blared from that old Juke

Glen Miller and Count Basey

Benny Goodman and the Duke

That's how I recall the US GI's

When they first appeared in town

They came over here to help us

And they didn't let us down.

25. CLOSE TO DROWNING – 1943

Whilst playing out with the gang

Near a rust red flowing stream

Trickling from those iron stone hills

Where industry had been

I tried to climb a nearby tree

That overhung the brook

And crawled along a narrow branch

Just to have a look

At what the rest were up to

Playing by the stream

When suddenly the branch gave way

I fell off with a scream

Head first into that iron red mud

I couldn't move at all

I found my mind was drifting

But my friends had seen me fall

As they grabbed my back and hauled me out

And with an anguished cry

An iron red figure ran for home

Shouting. 'Oh God will I die.'

My mother angry at my state

As I came through the door

Shouted. 'Get those ruddy clothes off

-you are ruining my floor'

No sympathy did I receive

Although I nearly drowned

Just a tumble in a hot bath

While mother scrubbed and frowned

I learned a lesson on that day

To look out where you tread

Check every branch that you climb on

Or you will end up red or dead.

26. THE UNION JACK RULES – 1943

As pavement artists we excelled

When playing in the street

Drawing hopscotch layouts

Or silly faces on concrete

But of all the drawings we like to do

Was to convert the nasty swastika

By simply changing this ugly sign

To one we would prefer

We'd draw lines in the spaces

And St Andrews Cross went back

To change that rotten old swastika

Into our country's Union Jack

27. THE GANG AT LARGE – 1943

Our gang made the headquarters

During the holidays

In an abandoned old stone crusher

There we'd spend our summer days

The buildings were of rusting steel

There was danger always near

With an open tank of old black tar

From which we'd always steer

We would climb a metal structure

To a room right at the top

With corrugated roof and sides

And there we'd sit and swop

Our lead soldiers and our 'ciggy' cards

An aircraft with bent wings

A model car with rubber wheels

Favourite conkers with the strings

We'd talk about when we grew up

Perhaps as soldiers of the King

Or maybe a mechanical engineer

Designing the most amazing thing

Some said they would be miners

Following fathers down the pit

And spend life working at the coal face

In tunnels dimly lit

The days spent at the old crusher

Playing out our fantasy

With games so full of innocence

When Kids could play out free

28. LEARNING TO SWIM – SUMMER 1943

Without the irons my legs were weak

But swimming was my goal

And I knew while in the water

I'd float with weightless self-control

Wellington Baths were far away

So for a swim we'd go

To a pool we knew as Waxalls

With all the gang in tow

Some of us were learning

Others were quite good

So they would keep an eye on us

So that we all understood

We couldn't do any stupid things

For this was a dangerous place

It had a muddy bottom

And weeds would interlace

Around our legs in places

So we had a special spot

Where close to the bank there were no weeds

And if anyone forgot

And wandered into weed beds

They'd be quickly pulled away

So this was the place we learned to swim

On many a sunny day

But one day as we splashed about

A thunderstorm came by

Lightning flashed and thunder roared

Across a darkened sky

We hastened out and quickly dressed

Before the rain began

Trying to avoid the lightning flash

As to our homes we ran

I never told my parents

That I went into that pool

Without my heavy leg irons on

Disobeying every rule

But in that muddy weed filled pool

With unsupported limb

I achieved my first ambition

By learning how to swim

29. DIGGING FOR VICTORY – 1943

The garden was our larder

During wartime rationing

We grew all kinds of vegetables

All seasons through to Spring

My Grandad was the expert

He'd dig our plot each year

Then plant the seeds in long straight lines

I'd watch the seeds appear

In Summer came the salad crops

Ripe tomatoes, lettuce leaves

Celery and beetroot

And large red radishes

We'd water lines of garden peas

And watch the shells grow fat

Runner beans would flower and grow

With green pods long and fat

My Grandad would prepare a trench

To put potatoes in

And I would halve and place them there

With a generous manuring

And in the Autumn we would pick

The fruits of all our labours

Cabbages, onions, potatoes, leeks

Even give some to the neighbours

It kept us fed throughout the war

With fresh veg for the table

So 'Dig for Victory' became the call

In our wartime timetable.

30. BIRMINGHAM IS BLITZED - 1943

Father took us for a walk

On what were once old slag heap mounds

Now blanketed by nature

With tall grass and birdsong sounds

As we approached a hillock close to dusk

Hurrying home to bed

A raid began on Midland towns

Again the clouds above were red

Nazi Bombers over Birmingham

Had set the place ablaze

Lighting up the night sky

In a hellish fiery haze

It must have been a heavy raid

Though we could hear no sound

Just a vast red canopy

Reflecting fires that lit the ground

My father said we must get back

Bedtime was drawing near

But I just thought of the 'Brummy' folk

Who I knew had much to fear

With no home to go to

Where would they sleep tonight?

But 'Brummy" folk are resilient

They would stand and fight

They'd take all Fritz could throw at them

Even without sleep

They'd keep the factories going

A promise they would keep

31. HOW A TANK CROSSED A ROUNDABOUT – 1943

I was near a place called Humbers

Close to the Army Store

When suddenly from in the camp

There came a mighty roar

A tank came slowly through the gates

And turned into the road

It headed for the roundabout

As it approached it slowed

I saw it couldn't get around

But it didn't stop

It carried on straight over

As if mounting a hilltop

Bushes and trees were pushed aside

The tracks tore up the grass

As vehicles stopped and drivers stared

To watch the big tank pass

It continued over on it's way

Leaving quite a mess

Mud and debris on the road

From this unauthorised access

When I returned there some months later

The roundabout had changed

Concrete tracks had been laid across

And the whole place re-arranged

It had now become the usual thing

For tanks to cross each day

But thanks to the driver of that tank

Who opened up the way.

32. A WALK TO IRONBRIDGE -1943

My father suggested on his rest day

We'd walk to the first iron bridge

So we caught a bus to Madeley

And set off o'er the ridge

And down the hill to Ironbridge

Walking all the way

Soon we reached the Derby factory

Where we stopped - for it neared midday

There we ate our sandwiches

Leaning over the factory wall

The yard had several brand new tanks

Just waiting for the call

For the Army to take delivery

And send to their personnel

They'd take them to the war zones

And give the Nazis hell

While we stood and watched this spectacle

Another tank appeared

Manufactured in this famous place

Where iron forging was pioneered

Then we went on to see the first iron bridge

Which spanned the river wide

A masterpiece of ironwork

It filled us all with pride

We arrived home tired that evening

Our legs and feet were sore

It had been a long and arduous walk that day

But what great things we saw

33.PLANE CRASH ON THE WREKIN - SPRING 1944

My father a Police War Reserve

In the Shropshire Constabulary

Came home one night so very tired

And couldn't face his tea

A plane had crashed and he was there

With service ranks all seeking

The bits and pieces of the aeroplane

Around a hill known as the Wrekin

He never mentioned the brave crew

Who'd lost their lives that day

Nothing more of the tragedy

Would my father say

The 'Journal' told the story

Much later in the week

The tragic loss of Naval aircrew

Who'd crashed close by that peak

Who knows what they had faced that day

Recovering those brave men

Who had given their lives in wartime

Close by that forest glen.

War affected every one

Whether home or far away

It shook their fathers and mothers

On that eventful day

(To the memory of Sub Lt Robert Charles Reeder and Lt Commander Watson Royal Naval Air Service who died that day).

34. A BRUSH WITH A WASPS NEST – 1944

Every day we walked to school

About a mile away

I was a bit of a slow coach

When I went to school that day

As I clumped along in my leg irons

I approached an old brick wall with care

For someone had disturbed a wasps nest

And some angry wasps were there

Suddenly my face was stung

Then my lips and ears and back

I tried to run as fast as I could

To avoid the wasp attack

I managed to escape the throng

And reached the school quite late

I entered my own classroom

The teacher appeared irate

But then she saw my swollen face

And told a monitor to deal with things

While she took me to the rest room

And gently treated all those stings

Then she asked the head teacher

If I could be allowed to go

This was agreed and off I went

Walking very slow

This time I kept away from the wall

Where the wasps nest had been stirred

When my Grandma saw my swollen face

She asked what had occurred

I spent the day recovering

The swelling soon went down

But when I returned to school next day

I felt just like a clown

But this soon changed within the class

For they knew as the day went by

I had been cared for by Miss Johnson

So my 'street cred' went sky high

35. BUILDING CAMPS – 1944

Behind our house there was a field

Where we could roam so free

We'd dig a hole the sides were square

Camouflaged with branches from a tree

And no one would know that we were there

Playing our different games

We'd pretend we were special agents

Giving ourselves nicknames

We'd be hiding from the Nazis

Out to get us before Tea

One of us would keep a look out

And we worked out ways of staying free

Sometimes we'd light a campfire

Bring potatoes there to cook

We'd place them in the ashes

And sit and wait and look

When burnt black we'd drag them out

Hoping they were baked

We'd remove all traces of the blackened skin

Until the Potato had been flaked

Then we'd taste the delights within

Taking care not to burn our lips

These were *our* cooked potatoes

Better than any chips

Sometimes they were raw and crunchy

Others soft and sweet

But none of us complained at all

To us this was a treat

And then one day my sister

Was left to tend the fire

And as she piled the twigs on

The flames rose higher and higher

Soon they had caught the outside grass

Before long the fire had spread

To a nearby corn field

My sister filled with dread

Ran shouting to a house nearby

And the fire alarm was raised

And for calling out the Fire Brigade

It was the perpetrator they praised

The Fire Brigade soon on the scene

Fire out the corn field saved

It hadn't spread so very far

They didn't know she'd misbehaved

We didn't light fires after that

One scare was enough it seems

And our craze of camp building ended there

Lost in a field of dreams

36. AN ENCOUNTER WITH GIPSIES – 1944

My friend Billy and I spent summer days

Trying our hand at fishing

With a stick rod, line and bent pin hook

We'd sit by the canal just wishing

That with worms we'd catch a nice large fish

But tiddlers took our bait

And as we put them in the jam jar

We'd shout and celebrate

So by the early afternoon

We had caught a dozen fish

We decided then to throw them back

For they wouldn't make a dish

And as we made our way back home

We passed a Gipsy camp

Where several wooden vans were parked

Set on a grassy ramp

Their horses grazed in a field nearby

Tied to wooden posts

A fire was alight in the centre ground

And sat there all engrossed

Three Gypsy ladies making pegs

Splitting willow sticks from nearby trees

One sat there cutting little strips

From a tin can on her knees

Another shaved and paired the sticks

She wrapped the small tin strips around

And fastened it with a tiny nail

So it was firmly bound

We stood there fascinated

At they work they undertook

Then they noticed we were interested

120

Saying 'Come and have a look'

We had been warned about the Gipsy folk

How they took young kids away

But we found these folk so very kind

As they passed the time of day

They offered us a cup of tea

And showed us things they made

Baskets, pegs and lucky heather

Which in nearby towns they'd trade

We felt it time to set off home

For there was a sudden change in weather

But before we left they gave us both

A lucky piece of heather

As we ran home in the pouring rain

We had seen a different side

Romany folk in honest toil

Weren't people to deride

37. THE VISIT – 1944

Apart from losing our London home

We'd got away scot free

But terrible news was to reach us

In 1943

My youngest Aunty Brenda

Was working on Munitions

One day she reached for a detonator

Under unstable conditions

The result was a huge explosion

She was blinded and terribly maimed

A most unfortunate circumstance

For which no-one could be blamed

She lost the lower part of her right arm

Her face was badly pitted

And after a long time in a hospital

A prosthetic arm was fitted

After a time in convalescence

At St Dunstan's learning Braille

She was transferred up to Shropshire

Near Church Stretton's lovely vale

Then in June of '44

My Mother said one day

'Tomorrow we're visiting Aunty 'B'

…so you can't go out and play.

We'll have to catch three buses

..and we haven't got much time.'

So the next day round about eight o clock

We joined a bus queue line

The first stop was in Wellington

Where the Shrewsbury bus we caught

But as we reached a place called Atcham

The bus came to a halt

Military Police were on the road

Waving traffic down

We wondered what was going on

Because we had to get to town

Mum said we'd miss our connexion

If we stayed here far too long

It seemed there was nothing we could do

But wait with the rest of the throng

Suddenly there was a rumbling sound

From the direction of some trees

And a huge Flying Fortress rose

Lifting on the breeze

It was followed by another

And another in the rear

The aircraft flying so low

We could see the crew so clear

And so the flight continued

'Till all the planes had gone

We raised a cheer for those brave lads

And the mission they were on

The bus at last was allowed to move

Got to Shrewsbury just before

The bus moved off to Stretton

And we could relax once more

Whilst travelling round the bypass

We couldn't believe what we saw

For lined up all along the road

Tanks and vehicles by the score

It was ages before we'd passed them

And the bus continued on

Arriving at Church Stretton

And the journey was all done

We left the bus and began to walk

Towards St Dunstan's house

At the top of a hill we rested

In a church lynch gate we sat

Then my mother started laughing

And gave her knees a pat

We wondered why the laughter

Then she pointed and then cried

'That dustbin by the churchyard wall

..has 'Old Bones' on the side

We saw the joke

And laughed out loud to see

That dustbin with 'Old Bones' inscribed

Next to a cemetery

We soon arrived at the house

Where only nurses there could see

We were sat down in the sitting room

And asked if we'd like tea

My aunt came in and greeted us

Her poor face was a sight

With pitted cheeks and hollow eyes

It gave me quite a fright

Her blouse had a pinned up sleeve

Where once her arm had been

But for all her tragic injuries

She stood there like a Queen

Then she came over to me

Her left hand touched my jaw

And with her fingers scanned my face

I guessed that's how she saw

'He looks just like you Doris

…he certainly has your nose.'

My Mother gently nodded

And said quietly 'I suppose'.

My Aunt scanned both my sisters

And said how pretty they were that day

Then a nurse came in to the room

With tea and biscuits on a tray

My Aunt insisted on pouring

She said she had learnt a way

Of pouring tea into the cup

Without spilling it on the tray

She put her finger on the edge of the cup

And when the tea got near

She told us all to shout 'stop!'

And took her finger clear

She continued filling all the cups

Using the same technique

And followed up by pouring milk

Then settled down to speak

We spoke together for half an hour

While we ate biscuits and drunk tea

And then Mum asked us to play outside

While she talked to Aunty 'B'

We went outside in the garden

And had quite a surprise

It was full of men with bright blue suits

Sporting white shirts and bright red ties

These men had been blinded in the War

And brought back from the front

They were here for convalescence

Their blindness to confront

One patient listening to us talk

Turned round and with a smile

Said.' You kids come from London

-you can tell it by a mile'.

Then he said 'You 'eard the latest news

-we've landed troops in France

-and now we'll give old Adolph hell

-we'll make those 'Jerries' dance'

And that's how we heard of 'D' Day

On a visit to 'Aunty 'B'

And those lessons that I learned that day

Would always remain with me

And how people can overcome

The tragedies of life

By facing a life of blindness

After their terrible wartime strife

38. THE 'DOODLE-BUG – 1944

One day whilst shopping in Oakengates

We came upon a crowd

Standing round the Council Offices

All chatting rather loud

Mother asked why all the fuss

To which a lad replied.

'They've found a ruddy 'Doodle-Bug'

-and they've got it parked outside'

On a notice in the entrance

For everyone to see

Was a large poster display

With 'Wings For Victory'

They were making a collection

For our brave boys in the air

And to bring the people closer

They were showing something rare

It was an unexploded 'Doodle-Bug'

From which they'd taken the H.E.

And they were now proudly displaying it

For everyone to see

There was no propeller

Just a strange round tube like thing

Fitted on a long metal body

On either side a wing

When later I was older

I learned the havoc it could reap

Many falling out the sky

Turning streets into a smouldering heap

People looking skyward

When they heard the spluttering sound

Wondering when the engine stopped

Where it would come to ground

The 'Doodle-Bug' to me as a child

Was a funny looking thing

But I've learnt about this weapon of war

And the suffering it could bring

39. WINTER SPORTS ON THE INCLINE - 1944

The snow was deep that winter

And my father made a sledge

And so we had to test it out

On a suitable hilly ledge

The best place we could think of

Was Wrockwardine Wood close by

An ancient Canal Incline Plane

On which barges used to ply

We soon climbed up to the top of the bank

With our new sledge in tow

The snow ideal for sledging

We couldn't wait to have a go

My father then insisted

He should try the new sledge out

So he lay down on the flat top

And shot off with a shout

The sledge went flying down the hill

Father clinging to the top

He found as he reached the bottom

That sledge refused to stop

Then suddenly without warning

The sledge began to lift

My father legs akimbo

Flew straight into a drift

He stood up laughing loudly

He had survived a dangerous ride

We were relieved he was OK

And saw the funny side

The rest of our day out sledging

Was full of laughs and fun

We would never forget the day our father

Hit a snowdrift on the run

40. V.E. DAY - MAY 1945

'It's just been on the radio

…the surrender was announced.

…Our boys will soon be coming home

…the Nazis have been trounced'

My mother so excited

Had rushed into the room

'Now we can look to the future

…It will all be over soon.

They only have to beat the Japs

…then we'll all be free.

…Gran you put the kettle on

…and we'll toast those boys with tea.'

And that is how I heard the news

Of victory that May

Then huge bonfires were lit

To celebrate that day

But never forget those brave souls

That gave their lives for you and me

To ensure a life of happiness

And a country that stayed free.

41. PEACE AT LAST - 1945

The woods of Shropshire wondrous wild

Through which I'd wander as a child

And do the most exciting things

Like climbing trees and imagining

I was a sailor out at sea

Aloft in a crow's nest of greenery

Searching a sky line of sea green hills

Alert to the sound of high pitched trills

Of Skylarks rising oh so high

Ascending till they touched the sky

And when I'd tired of this magic show

I would climb down the tree to the depths below

And wander through an imaginary sea

Of waist high bluebells drawing me

Through a gate and down a track

To a field of grass where I'd lay on my back

And gaze in reverie at the sky

Sucking a honey tipped piece of Rye

Where cotton wool clouds blown by the breeze

Formed tigers, bears and chimpanzees

And that fluttering Lark that flew so free

Now etched so clear in my memory

Are part of those days so long ago

Just sweet memories that ebb and flow

Within my old but active brain

Recalling my Shropshire youth again

To-day, as we celebrate victory, I send this personal message to you and all other boys and girls at school. For you have shared in the hardships and dangers of a total war and you have shared no less in the triumph of the Allied Nations.

I know you will always feel proud to belong to a country which was capable of such supreme effort; proud, too, of parents and elder brothers and sisters who by their courage, endurance and enterprise brought victory. May these qualities be yours as you grow up and join in the common effort to establish among the nations of the world unity and peace.

George R.I.

Printed in Great Britain
by Amazon